THE
APOCALYPSE
OF EVE

Aurora of the Philosophers

THE APOCALYPSE OF EVE

ALANA EISENBARTH

THE APOCALYPSE OF EVE

Light Realm Books
Copyright © 2019 Alana Eisenbarth

Cover image photo "Spooky Tree" by wyldraven (Deviant Art)

Text set in FF Milo
Printed in the United States of America.

ISBN-13: 978-0-9914649-4-4

ONLY TAKE HEED TO THYSELF, AND
KEEP THY SOUL DILIGENTLY, LEST
THOU FORGET THE THINGS WHICH
THINE EYES HAVE SEEN, AND LEST
THEY DEPART FROM THY HEART.

DEUTERONOMY 4:9

"And let us instruct him in his sleep to the effect that she came from his rib, in order that his wife may obey, and he may be lord over her."

Then Eve, being a force, laughed at [the Rulers'] decision. She put mist into their eyes and secretly left her likeness with Adam. She entered the tree of knowledge and remained there. And they pursued her, and she revealed that she had gone into the tree and become a tree.

On the Origin of the World from the Nag Hammadi Library

The Apocalypse (Revelation) of Eve

BOOK 4

WITHOUT GOD, NATURE IS A DEAD CREATURE.

KARL VON ECKARTSHAUSEN

WHOEVER HAS COME TO UNDERSTAND THE WORLD HAS
FOUND ONLY A CORPSE, AND WHOEVER HAS FOUND A
CORPSE IS SUPERIOR TO THE WORLD.

THE GOSPEL OF THOMAS

ELIJAH

We walk in the light, and then turn away back to the world of forms. It is prescribed. I am still trying to make peace with this, with being here and knowing, trying to understand again my role when there is only light, my memory of it, a veil dropped, what I have chosen.

How wrong we are here. How we have gotten it so wrong. What powers we have, and yet, our greatest seems our power to destroy. And so I decimate the world in a book, having only written what has been asked, what has been revealed, what I have seen. I will be asked to restore it, I suppose, to redeem us, to rebuild. (They must ask me to rebuild it.) For now I wait, watching the praying mantis, watching the great blue heron take to flight, watching and awaiting my turn...

conscience. Do you remember, the domed walls, the skull, entering the third door of the cathedral, this body cage at first and cave and then something resurrected, stretching and then declension?

aurora. Me pushing and shoving, but the angel said,— no, it wasn't the angel but the woman we'd burned who said, "Remember this. You will need it."

conscience. Remember everything at the council of the eternal ones where you sat divided and returned. Remember Elijah looking on, purple robed. Come.

aurora. He one of three, but I was frightened and

returned to the world without you, and now again you come for me because I ask, beseech, implore.

I see myself in the cave, where skull has widened into sepulcher, a tomb a kingdom long, and I am here awaiting the hand of God and yet not waiting but exploring what it is to remember we were sent for something. Yes, this I have always known. Verses come through me in exploration of a human form: the woman, the eternal feminine, this dark bird in me who is but my might and the might of the Father, separate and eternal, a being ravaged and fed and yet chasten and pure in a way light poured through garment might know none of this and all at once, the way light contain color, spectrum, song. Oh how to live is to be human to be God and a story as it unfolds. And I am afraid this is all I am as I settle in the light ambition gone. It is as you have prescribed, one gone through hell, a prophet dragged, unseen and seeing, all of these pieces, elusive parts of the whole.

And how one might see in a point an intersection of parts, in a point, the motion of number, a line, a sphere, a plane, the elusive eternity of the whole.

I have seen our end and a path beyond, the path beyond consciousness I was born with of our redemption: a vision superseding apocalyptic drum. I had forgotten this until now, my life a recalling of what is has been comes. As I stand at the end, it is to this vision I rise, knowing I've been here all along, knowing while I make it, not all make it.

THE STAIRCASE

There is a staircase chamber to chamber. I close my eyes and follow its golden light to the bend, the lowest point in white light, for it is easy now to traverse from here to there, to make here there, to feel you within me to feel beyond. There is buoyancy, ascension, and yet what would levitate here on a plane of light within a world of forms, what knows itself has always known, what wars and dread and beauty, a sanctuary, a holy land inside the head, a history, a pummelling, a cistern, a sledge. And now? We can't but this.

And so I begin again to tell you the story, to tell us the story, before the golden light sinks over memory over the scenes opening out across lands and times all at once existing in the imaginative realm as but dreams of a human dying, a human sleeping its way into oblivion, a human I am not to force awake but to walk by perchance it sense a prickle of sand on its skin, a serpent in the depths stirring.

And I will be Elijah, the will of God willing the will of Ham to its end.

THE FALL

While you sleep the alchemist is wringing her hands in an underworld cave. She has learned a secret that will take us out of this night.

Think of a girl drowning in a well, drowning in a garden. She surfaces, keens for what she has witnessed in the abyss of the world. She belongs to neither water nor land, land nor water but drowns and surfaces, surfaces and drowns until the pervading images become one, until there is no longer well or garden. Now this is a story. Garden should raise hackles. The Garden, yes, where it all began, and yet everything they told you was wrong. This is a story and that was a story. And yet we have reached an end where it just might be possible for you to see now what you had not, that you might believe and in believing... but we haven't gotten to that yet.

In medias res, they tell us. Enter the serpent, oh happy, happy wraith.

What if one day you woke to a serpent rising in your head? What if that serpent writhed and stretched and caused your skull to expand? Adam would tell you to take something to suppress it, but you are an observer, a seeker, not touching so much as being touched, so you let it unravel within you although at times you cannot stand. Its weight is strong in you, blackening your vision as it coils behind your eyes.

"Baby, take something," Adam says, steadying your arm. But the snake has begun to move you and to speak. It tells you to get to the west coast where you will meet a Sufi man. It tells you to hold out your hand until you feel it so full and heavy with promise you almost believe, almost believe you will get there it moves you so, yet you procure no funds in the coming days, so you do not go to California. You stay with Adam in the garden.

WHERE I DROPPED THE LIGHT

At the cusp of the world, there is a rock, a boulder, just beyond an aperture of sky. Here, my husband will wait for me on an afternoon drenched in sunlight in a clearing in the woods where the path has taken us.

"Go ahead. But hurry. It'll be dark soon," he says.

On the face of the rock, comes the gloaming, the valley and firmament a radiant mass of quivering peace that reaches into my chest to claim me. In acquiescence, I step into the sky, sealing a covenant with the tranquil light, my mind clear, knowing, unknowing.

How can one explain one's death in a star of light?

∞

Manley? How long have you been on your knees, anchoring my body to this crag, tears welling in your eyes, scarlet with restraint? You, my love, on whom I fall in a heap as a bird passes over the sky. I am a blanket of golden song, a pitch eternally slung into flight, levitating, suspended from a dream. My heart opens to your body, damp and velvet. We move the air, shove it into us and beyond, our chests filling with wind and wild gathering, your hand searing my waist.

∞

I have frightened him. He loves and cannot love me. In his words, I gather myself from the sky and attempt to assemble a human form. Light no longer moves. He is standing above me now, extending his hand. Yet how can I rise when I am disparate parts in a valley?

"I can't love this," he says, gesturing to me, the rock. "Where were you going? Are you a child?"

I am blood pooled on a rock.

"Hey. Talk to me." He nudges my thigh with his boot. "Say something. Take your head from the clouds."

There is light, and there is darkness, a body in ablution, letting him see it, water leaking over an abysmal wall.

In the car he no longer wants to hear what I have to say. What I have done is treacherous, which is when I begin to see the rivalry between him and God, which is when I begin to see him as Adam, which is when I begin to see everything, and that is how I know we have gotten it wrong. It was your story, not mine, Adam. Mine was something else. In mine the serpent wakes something. In mine begins a journey, for as soon as I fall, division. And then I know.

I am losing you in my story, however, and I am losing God.

SONG OF DARKNESS (LIGHT)

How a human soul might be eroded like a canyon for the sake of beauty on this plane and on another growth, ascension. Here: evolution, there: regeneration in the light. How eroding would sound, ululating perpetually at the same pitch that it might strike resonance within you in the well. And if you could descend through the center of your being, I would be there holding out the light that you might see the animals, that you might feel, that you might open your heart and in opening descend. How the soul would be this well of resonating sound, how it would carry a cry ever vacant, ever swept clean in the eroding, for the eroding would move particle in wind, displacing. How this would go on forever. How the poet would tack this cry to a page, pages, the ego obeisant, busy with its task, tacking, hammering, banging, here a verse nailed shut at its unveiling. And how the heart might not open as it did, having been nailed shut so many times.

We create the dark in ourselves and the light.

∞

The snake within me surfaces, observes, and then retreats back inside. How shall I understand all of this? I am in awe and in limbo. I have to believe they will come. The ones who were promised, the ones who came off of me like leaves at my birth. But perhaps an oracle does this, scatters what is later to be recollected as she lives a code of scrawl. How a tree of life would yield.

THE ALCHEMIST

I hold the heart chakra open until I would collapse, un-practiced in this art, learning as I go. Adam's diatribe is fierce when we get home. On the landing at the top of the stairs, he clenches his fists and beats at the door frame. *Oh, that it were you instead.* Yes, a resume of broken ex-perience. The boss man's none. What have I done? Six thousand years with no pension, no nest egg, no job se-curity or thought to the future. No money. And now this. Was I trying to kill myself?

I saw God, Adam. But I can't tell him this.

"You are old. I am sorry to say it, but you just don't get it. This writing that you do, this speaking to the divine... If God exists, where's the money, Ror? He should support you, no? Frankly, I'm tired of it. Get a job like the rest of us."

Under the bell, I stand with legs of rippled water. What he is saying says nothing of me; what he is saying de-scribes a girl with a song he hasn't heard. We are a water cannon, what could obliterate this human form, yet we abscond.

"Horses and rabbits, prosperous signs. I don't want to hear any more of this trash. Yes, trash." Having vocalized this last point, he is brazen, and when it comes, he squeezes my cheeks in his hand.

"I came back for you." I say, shaking. There once was a

white bird with my name.

"What? Oh, that nonsense! I'm all wrong for you, Ror. You've convinced me if that is what you've been trying to do."

"No, Adam."

We are speaking over each other in this white cage, this jar. I am touching his lips to silence his mouth, balling his shirt in my hands.

"I was wrong. Please. I betrayed you. I can see now what I couldn't. Please. I didn't know."

"Why don't you go stay with your mother?"

"For how long, Adam? I can't, I won't go. If I go, you mean forever. I can hear it."

—

"How could I have been so naïve?"

He is deflated. "What if I hadn't been there? What if you had taken that step off the rock?"

∞

He writes me from work that I should go close down the heart. These are not his words but mine. I will tear it from my chest, pierce it through with a butcher blade. In my skull what has expanded is being crunched into a box, wadded and pressed and shoved back inside. That I can be here in the world, I must put back God. If I lose Adam now, I have nothing.

The next few days call for penitence. I am ravaged, obsequious, tamed. I could puke up my life. What would have been lost is desperate to wear his flesh, to touch and paw and be inside. To swing across his ribs.

His face is pulled, worn, I notice when he falls asleep in my arms. My love has done this. It cannot be as it was, he says on getting up. He is still thinking he will leave me. He needs time. I should go.

∞

I am half a body no heart. I cry out when an angel appears and shoots a barb of light into my throat that dries out the words of my plaint. I gawk at the flash of gold that is no longer and sink onto my elbows in awe.

How close they are to come to me. How close that realm is now. And that is how I know we have gotten it wrong.

BE NOT AFRAID

Be not afraid, say the angels in the bible, but I am petri-
fied, obligated now to testify to some arcane dream.
That I have been visited twice by seraphim, shot twice
in the throat requires something. There will be no return to the paradigm being upheld. How could I return,
knowing now what I know?

And yet nothing has been verbalized. I ask myself if
it had, if I had heard the angels say, *Go now into the
world with my message, which is...* would it be easier?
But I know it would not, for there exists such disparity
between phenomena and the spiritual realm that a harbinger's words might be as quickly forgotten as a message relayed sanguine.

In a dream this night my hand swells, the band choking
the life out of it. It will need to be removed. I wake up
in a sweat, knowing what is being asked. But he is
mine, and we, too, share a covenant. I will bargain for
him. The bible shows that I can do this. It has to do with
perseverance and the purity of will. But I am getting
ahead of myself.

WHAT THEY BROUGHT WITH THEM, THE ANGELS

Every scene within the holy book will be enacted in your life, over and over, over centuries, until you reach the end, until you have played every part, until John, Moses, Elijah, Jacob, Eve... These were not historical figures but states of consciousness. This is what they were trying to tell us, these prophets of old.

On reaching Elijah, you will be given a task. On reaching God, it is done. Some will step into the light and be gone from us. Others will be returned. The more who awaken the easier it will be for the rest, once we have forged a path. Those with the staircase or ladder, those who have broken the seals, those who have sat beneath the tree, beheld the night visions, seen God. These will lead us. It will not be long.

Jesus was buried in the place of the skull. When he rises within, you will know.

Until then, let us pretend the prophet is dead. Let us pretend we have exhumed these fascicles from a tomb, merely to be present in evolving this thing, growing what we are, becoming conscious, remembering that what happens would have been prescribed in a book. According to scripture, that it be done. That there would be something calling me back to the world I'd been out of for so long. That it would take disremembering, berating, and depredating. That Adam alone would know how. That I would give myself over, knowing an end and beginning, knowing what was to come.

Stars break around me, and I know my path as God. Some of us have snakes in our bellies. Some of us have come for the end.

aurora. Oh how does the one returned recount where she has been?

conscience. To carry the light is to carry the darkness. Where are you?

aurora. At the end of a world without end.

What do you think you have that I need? *A male voice—world.*

aurora. A vision. A way out of the darkness and greed.

world. Tell me.

aurora. You won't believe.

NATURE, A DEAD CREATURE

It is one of those scenes in which time slows. One senses and in sensing sees from outside the truck, the wheels as black clocks running backward. The bend in the road is lit, the low brush along the roadside illuminated as the opossum steps out, a gleaming suitor to the stage. Quicksilver he tiptoes the asphalt, this dapper, clandestine walker of night's grounds.

There is the clamor of luggage being stowed in the carriage: the opossum rolled beneath the wheels we go on.

"I'm sorry," Manley whispers. "I saw it too late to react."

I am quiet. Something is wrong. "Do you feel anything?"

"I feel bad, of course. I didn't mean to hit it," he says defensively.

"No, that's not what I mean. Does it feel different to you at all?" But why should anything have changed for him? It was my ascension and fall.

"I killed an animal. How should I feel?"

"It's just, I feel nothing. It could have been cardboard, a doll."

∞

aurora. The light is gone. Open it. Open me. Come.
conscience. They were here for your birth.
aurora. Who?
conscience. The ones you called watchers, the wise-men who'd come.

∞

What if the fall were simply our forgetting the God in us? Why can't I say I as God? As a creature that recognizes in its human form a unique beauty? What will never exist this way again and yet whose existence is perpetual?

BOOK 5

Step away from the others and I shall tell
you the mysteries of the kingdom.

THE GOSPEL OF JUDAS

Things I had always questioned, how one might know an angel's name, how one might definitively say it is like this. Or like this. We die in fire. We are infinite, immortal. There are 49 stages in the journey of the soul. That an angel might appear no larger than a human hand. For its distance?

LET THE WORLD DIE

It was not at all what we had thought, not at all what we'd been told. This was the world we'd wake up to: cutthroat and red-push ejaculation. Easy assertion of the impossibility of all things. They had their -cides down to a system so that it was to be a thorough cleansing. Few thought now. Those who did begrudged them a soul to the vocation.

From all where were we going?

∞

Anima had had enough. The grief god had her. And now? There were some who were saying the light had gone out, some who were saying the worlds within had been tarnished, that it was not only the physical world of concrete forms that we were annihilating but the sacred underworld of spirits as well. They didn't know we had moved her.

LUMEN NATURAE

conscience. The deva was you, Aurora. No one removed the souls. It was a story you told yourself. We suffer. There is nothing to end this suffering but to turn to the light within.

∞

Rarely had I gone within with such intention. This plane was dark. Something had torn through and ravaged it. And in the murky yellow light, I came upon a bird or deva, a colossal form that had given its life. What more was here but this form in the darkness and a pale yellow light I cannot say. How can I explain how a body might know all at once the battle that had occurred and how this one was mortified?

I wanted to hold it in my arms if only because I could not stand its sadness, its empty despair. But dead things don't despair. I was despairing. I was the bird through the bird its wings my arms, and I was life but for its heaviness, lead-dead. I tried to move it knowing I had no right yet believing in grace and resurrection. But who am I to resurrect a bird into a dying world, and for what good?

These things did not occur to me but black pain, an annihilated soul.

aurora. One would have to have been annihilated to

know this.

conscience. It was why an angel. It was what you wanted to know.

aurora. Then I have not wronged you in choosing love?

conscience. That you returned to Adam? We gave you vision that you might see.

aurora. Then you still need me? I was afraid when there was nothing left. When light had left me.

conscience. Consciousness.

aurora. But the bridge in my throat. Is that the charge? Was the angel activating the throat chakra? Or was it simply to silence me? (I feel it tear, a segment hacked.)

THE SERAPH (FIRST VISITATION)

In answer to the question asked in dream a gilded creature riddled with wings appeared at ceiling height over
the foot of the bed. There the seraph lingered and I
mouth agape felt a dry, barbed ball shot into my gullet.
Then the golden figure was gone, and I returned to
sleep.

∞

conscience. Do not resist what comes naturally to
you, what comes peacefully, what gives you rest. What
is real is what you feel within you to be true. Do not let
this world tell you otherwise.

VISION

Negative space. What is body
to one sky to the other; what is
substance, vacancy;
orifices, animals climbing a mountain ever
in ascent, descending tentacles moving
stillness, again that form, anthodite: what grows
undisturbed in the darkness,
white beauty undiscovered then
maculate and stunted, defunct.

It is the moon again, a body men have walked.

HYLASTER

Webs cross my hands, trail my forearms. You are weaving me into the fireflies' green light, ascending over a yellow meadow beneath a turquoise sky. The moon is a golden ring in the burgeoning pink cumulus. A deer in the thicket slips

under the veil. Light rises
in sparks. There are no words,
the witness gone
dumb: what we have done
what we have done what we have
done. I am not to notice
the passing but the threads
that stretch across my arms,
the crown on my head, what the
angel shot into song. The jar tipped,
a womb, something begotten.

The spider and the gnats. Hylaster. Are you starting to see how this comes together?

Some of us have moved beyond the system, beyond this Caesar's world. I cannot explain how except that need catalyzed a new phase. Something was drawn: a gnat in wind, for when one sees a need for other, it comes, not in human ways but in ways meant for Gods. It is why the stretched head. There are some among us who've rolled the rock from the tomb.

ADAM'S WORK

She is in ecstasy, in a state beyond, taken where he cannot follow, so that he resorts to transgression, to degradation, the masculine power to defile and thus regain control.

Like this Adam calls me back to the body, to a woman I once was in the phenomenal world, a failure in a world of men, so that gravity replaces the light of God, shutting it out, eclipsing it. And in the fallacy, I stick fast, trapped again within a system flawed: the idea that I could die, or that what this world of his might recompense for God, that possession, or success, might mean anything.

THAT GOD WOULD BE THE TRANSGRESSOR

To become conscious again of our nakedness and our guise, to lift again the veils of this existence and know a god to be the transgressor, for there is wisdom on the ground where you left her. And there is a man dumb-founded for what he has become.

We had gotten it wrong. At the end was a snake and a woman with the courage to awaken not to the tale as they'd told it, but how it was, Adam complacent in the dream, she one with God, a serpent unfurling and coiling in her heart rising and tilting her waters over what was trickling down in deluge, saying to me come. Tip the bowl. You will know this has been a dream. On the underside of all we have known you will see.

We are what evolves us. The serpent unites us with God.

And so I was not to create but to apprehend, veils drawn, to be racked open, the pressure in the skull, the tremor of the head, palsy, the light.

DEFICIENCY

I couldn't see the beauty yet. Would it be inside the darkness? For the darkness was all around. This, another kind of darkness, one in which nothing shines, so that it is darkness devoid of the darkness of soul. Soul darkness has a purpose, a meaning.

conscience. In preparation for the end you took them out; made them soulless.

aurora. Adam's world. What would hurt more knowing? Is this why I could not feel it when the thing died, why it did not affect me to hear it beneath us, crushed?

conscience. Yes.

aurora. Take me out. I cannot be here.

conscience. You are visiting. Stave of light, you have come.

aurora. To see the world through his eyes! Oh shade of animal, cardboard throw, echelon! How empty it all seems, how arbitrary and meaningless. He'd have to be godless, soulless within. Within the observer would be nothing, so the world profane could be pillaged and raped.

conscience. Yes. Yes!

aurora. I don't understand these things.

A dragonfly alights on the windshield, and my heart will burst for love and wonder.

conscience. Do you get it now?

aurora. That some infuse our world with love, en-soul it; what we are would be reflected.

conscience. We took them out. You always knew it would be like this.

aurora. Anima mundi under the world where I stay with her through the night—night being world asleep, night being as long as they'd make it.

conscience. As long as who'd make it?

How perception strips of essence, deep down things, this essence being light. One apperceptive of this essence would assume a nexus with all sentient form, so that life macerated into the stream, the life force leaving a body would be felt by spiritual human, assimilated by the creature within. I felt no sadness, for there was no light, no spirit, for there was nothing. Take me out, I pleaded. But it wasn't a place but a state of consciousness to ascend.

Whatever you give credence to, it is everything.

So that I only need look at her to claim her.

∞

There is an angel in the dregs of coffee, half dark half light. Inside of her is a figure, a woman. Me? I am everything. Light flows into the back of an animal. The animal is the earth.

PERMANENCE IMPERMANENCE

That we took the soul and transported it and then not, neither fixed nor stagnant, it needed to be like this: a girl relinquishing all for a creature, for in the selflessness of the act a new soul was born.

It is why we cannot hold to things, why we must live detached, knowing permanence to be impermanence, knowing the illusion of every state we pass in and out of: a particle appearing disappearing: woman, serpent, tree. But some will not be ready for this yet, this line of reasoning.

The Jewish mystics gave warning: one should not proceed on this path alone, or attempt it without instructor or a pure heart or a sack of lead, a fat male, leaden sack. I do not remember their warnings, but I know they were right to convey them and to heed them, for all is treachery some days.

Today, however, I am infused with love and brilliance. There in the brazen light a chink in the ether, an eternal glare as the robed ones wait just beyond my human sight. I feel the warmth beneath their garb. How is it? I feel their breath, my breath on their skin. I am a council of elders. I am 64000 robed men. I have ascended the last rung of the ladder.

∞

Would you believe me if I told you the world was yours? That all that existed around you was yours: the wars yours, the birds yours, the beauty we reach, anima mundi, the divine. And will you forgive us, for there is no forgiveness? Ahh, there is only turning to the lover in love, and love is the father the prodigal embracing.

Hell will be the moment we see what we have done. And ascension this moment, too. Look, you are my foot. I wash my feet in ablution. Oh, my love, come. Let us drink the wine God has been saving for the end of the feast, this wedding of sun and moon.

And last night again before sleep, how the mouth behind my mouth was filled with tension, how something was wound through my lips, how there might have been a barrel at the center of my mouth around which a metal wire was strung, conductive and yet perhaps made of light. We produce the light in ourselves and the darkness.

DARKNESS

That one might hear and fulfill her charge when another has not. That my negligence might have left
something unfulfilled for the Sufi. That he might have
been calling to the one he'd woken, that he might have
needed her on this day as one needs votaries, adherents
to an ancient art.

How many times I have dashed myself on this rock
not to learn! I see and yet, the inefficacy of the apparatus. I retreat. You expand in me, dilated, not just in
my heart but my skull. One scolding, a tirade or brand-
ing when I should have taken her out, removed her like
you said. But I couldn't see a way without money, and I
had none, and so in this world I am a grasshopper.
What do you want with me?

Rack me not so. If I am a seer, then this was all in
preparation. The story had to end before it began. I have
to believe you went off to secure a destiny. All of the
signs abundance: the deer in the creep, the stallions,
the hare.

Sparks of light and that realm threatens to break
open on this. I feel the presence of other. How close you
all have come. Or how close I?

And how I have aged more this year than any other.

aurora. What is destroying is simultaneously creating anew in a glass jar whose lid you are removing with

the sky. The poison that kept coming through the po-ems—you knew.

conscience. Yes. The fall, your breaking with God. It is within you.

∞

Show me my place in this world. To have grown then to be pressed back into the skull, immured, and now to grow again. I feel tearing. Will you return to me? Take me out again. Make a place for me. I am no good at this world.

conscience. You want to destroy it as much as I do. It is why we removed the souls.

ONLY THE ASCENDED

conscience. If you knew how your descent might be perceived from the plane of light. What might ignite might in pain, your pain, be dashed, gained, garred with light. That might be its charge and its way. And on the Pennsylvania byway an animal, light drawn out. Look around you now. It is the same. What has been depleted, used. What grows according to human laws, what follows defunct: his reality a dead shell, a dapper, silver shade flattened to the asphalt. Sakla, blind god.

Human dies here. Only the ascended move on.

How light moves as you move among the world of forms. It is the light ascending within that gives you cause to think of yourself in levitation.

aurora. But I cannot feel it like I did.

conscience. It will return as you remember.

aurora. Cupidity taking a hand and leading it into ruin. Odiousness. What beauty come from pillage, proffer, appropriation of what is allowed the eye, plastic, polystyrene, at a pittance?

conscience. The system is collapsing. Remain outside.

THE SNAKE, ADAM, AND GOD

Vertigo on rising and the room goes black as the snake rises into the skull. We had gotten it wrong. The snake was an aspect of God in the self, an initiation which Adam hadn't the courage to engage. The idea was to know ourselves divided and to grow.

It was not about Man and his helper, male and female, good and bad, but about the beginning of a human journey, about Human dreaming something into existence, something of a self in love. For here we are the Garden and the God and the promise of the snake; God wanting to know itself, God's emanation. Separation and nexus, nonduality through dual form, what strives, a snake cut, ouroboros. God? I see you. God. A tree.

I have lived two thousand years this one.

ETERNAL RECURRENCE

How many times have we been here? How many times have I told myself this story? How many times have I heard your whisper in the wall as if it were not centuries or fathoms that kept us apart?

The night bird chips poison from the wind. A tin box expands. There are dogs in the distance.

What is the purpose of prophesy if not to warn? Then this was not prophesy but what was, world out of time.

I return to the hospital, human world depraved. Come back down to earth with me, my husband says. Would that I died there in God; that perhaps the racking of psyche and the emergence of Ego that occurred might precipitate chaos, that something broken and destroyed in the traverse ensue. Regardless, what lay dormant, ignorant in soporific glum was awake now, conscious, aware. But the spider, this Demiurge rising from the depths of nature, with what message had he come?

The more we seek the greater we become until the physical form must too expand, and so the hospital opens out into the desolate plane again where we are no more. I am at the end. You are not here. And I die and I die and I die. What you have done, meaning I did nothing, meaning we've been here before, and you knew it would be like this.

∞

Being dragged back into the world and berated, while holding tight to this realm; a harbinger sent to activate something in the throat. How the words rack the body. How something will be taken. How Ego cowers in the head. How something will be taken. How I hold peace in my heart beneath the bell, how I hold the visions of those sent, how the metal cage pierces the flesh, how the heart bleeds. How I lose consciousness and fall...

Laden with attributes of a temporal plan, I fall hard. Yet I remember the Garden, Adam. And the peace in my chest is unscathed. It centers and locates me beyond on an infrangible plane where I reside while human core is wounded. Synthesis. There will be moving beyond but not yet.

Adam knows not what he does. Were I to show him he would die to claim it all. Oh to become conscious for him would be death. To relinquish the sword... He will fight harder and destroy everything this time when he would only need to look at her, at what is feminine and divine, and see himself. Still he defiles, blind to shadow, so that I hold her away from him, away inside, but it is different this time. Adam is relentless, as if sensing what is at stake, and she in the stillness, absorbing the core, gathers her strength for emergence.

conscience. Don't you see that body is the body they made? They will defile it, and you will feel her pain.

ONE RETURNED AND UNSEEN

conscience. You asked to see. This is the world they have made.

aurora. But if I am to infuse it, wouldn't I need aid?

conscience. Oh how brightly you shine in the darkness.

aurora. And now you are mocking me.

conscience. Take your place on the ground.

aurora. How I could strip the veins from my arms not to be Human. If it were a cycle that had to play itself out, shouldn't I speak? Shouldn't the one who had seen something else, who knew another way, give voice to that plight?

conscience. That you could look on them with light and so change them; see deeply enough to ignite a transformation. That is all.

I hold the heart open but there are just these images that pass like cloud.

AURORA

I am holding open the metal box outside the door, the vial in my chest slipping on its slat of floor, emerald glowing in glass surrounded by lead. Manley beats at the door frame. *I could smash your stupid nothing head!* I hold my hand to my breast to secure the vial, to affirm its presence, unshaken still. As long as he does not see, for what he doesn't see, he cannot take from me.

I do not recognize until later that I would have brought him before me as a testament to my might, for to hold the peace within me, to hold the image of a transmogrified self against his diatribe, the beauty of a fallen god against a man would have been a necessary feat. But had I failed?

I see the scene: the crumpled body, a homunculus I came by that night, the god that spirit saved crawling back into the skull, an angel made, its body, the bodies of butterflies crunched into a watering can. Wounded wound, stave of light, an angel entering the bedroom, come to ignite the throat that you might traverse the realms less torturously. Setting fire to the bridge, the way back: a starred nexus...

Over the bed I see the tiny form, all gold and wings, no visage to behold, or figure of a body, just the release of a golden arrow caught in the throat, a dandelion gone to seed, and then sleep.

Afterward, making love to Manley, accepting his

flesh, my flesh. And how strangely biblical it all seems, my betraying him for God, his treachery an act, God here the transgressor in Manley's eyes.

∞

I am an ancient muse; fury takes my head.

Turkey vultures flit back and forth in the dormer, and I go down into the subterranean rooms of this house to my lab. Mason jars line the upper walls, some bursting vacant with song, others stuffed with tiny rags. Here a bird, a remnant of flight in a molting thing. Don't look so sad. I stroke his graying beak, his head lose in the socket leaning dead into my hand, detach the gnarled claw that has curled around my forefinger, and set him in the crook of the jar.

A spider tries to enter through the attic, its thick, ebony legs feeling their way around the ceiling panel, a god rapping at the door.

And I am sitting here with my stave of light...

conscience. Heart-wrenching my dear, but you must give that spear back to the salamander king.

I become aware of myself then in this cave of borrowed light.

conscience. Stolen, Aurora. Thieved. Pilfered. Robbed.

aurora. Okay. Okay. I hand the rod off to a surly looking elemental who then kisses me on the nose, drawing a sensation akin to sunburn.

I swallow the seeds and go into the darkness yet again, knowing the serpent, its power conjoined, its cunning and ascension.

Fire straw ignite. What when a God would want to destroy?

We have not seen, and so I am the woman in red at the top of the mountain waving the flag of her gown, the sun magnified to scorch her own, to set ablaze that you might see what comes of a woman rising from ash.

How little we've learned in the land of illusion.

There is the sense of failed urgency.

What matters to the dead but that they rise. And in the night, the council of 64000 speaking in your head. What have they said? What have they decided?

What you have done what you have done what you have done.

I sing it now, not knowing anything and yet knowing somehow all, always having known, waking to it. Recognizing myself in the dream first of Adam and now my own, stepping over the threshold and knowing that I have come here is of importance. Knowing sin to be what I deny of myself, acceptance of this world of forms, when what I am has grown beyond body, adumbrations beyond the veil.

Love, I have come not to lay myself down by your side but to love as a god loves. And so united, synthesized we go on. Me with the god in myself, what I am when you ask me what I am.

TO KNOW IT IS THERE

I have but to step forward into the house. I have only to feel the pure cold water easing from the bath, the concrete sink, how lovely deep you are! Abysmal. And the leaves falling in rust to the ground and the conifers conferring in the glass room, path beneath path, this world beneath world. Synthesis, you said, you speaking then to the others, the collective who we are.

And I know all you have done I have done.

EVE AND THE RULERS OF UNRIGHTEOUSNESS

There are some among us who don't belong to Adam but to God.

God raps at the brain, and a woman wrestles that God in the form of a bird, an angel, shoving it back down, breaking its wings that it might be caged in the skull, that she might live this play of world where Adam reigns and loves her, in a realm defunct, a whelp ever hanging from the stair.

But you don't know this story like I do, how a girl could be God, how a girl could come with a tireless spirit and be done, and then rise; witness herself in herself and rise to a higher plane.

When one seeks to understand the incomprehensible, the mind expands in response. God opens in us and welcomes expansion. This is no god of the patriarchy but Eros: the world through a star. What these Archons have told you is a lie. Get up and be more with me. Burn the world to ash and in burning, release. Do not be afraid. The you that exists around you can be unmade.

And in this paper animal, this deva on the ground, there would be no battle, no fight, no wresting or argumentation, simply a glance cast in love and reverence and what you see might transform.

The crystal child coming down.

aurora. So Human dies.

conscience. To be reborn as something else. It is why the ritual of protection.

aurora. The egg. You were preparing me. And those recordings perfectly aligned.

conscience. Trust and go on.

aurora. I die again. How can I not die knowing?

God whispers into the dragon's ear until the dragon lies down.

CONSENT

aurora. Veils drawn aside, one could see how the violence against women and earth had been sanctioned somehow; in the treatment of self, was consent. Servile compliance, every act against the better judgment reflects a desecrated world. And now?

conscience. We have come this way again. Understand on awakening how one returns to sleep.

Bluebirds flit back and forth before the window.

conscience. In nature, you return. Unclasp the heart box; let it be empty.

A moth enters the light on my pillow.

aurora. How redemptive when one releases herself from her own prison, for in her we see ourselves and know it is possible.

conscience. Tell the intellect to sleep, the Ego for now to nod off as I take you under and beneath.

aurora. Cave is the womb, the skull, the subconscious, a glass jar. And I see the snake now, this Ouroboros lifting its head, devouring, supplanting with fervor a species that one might become. Serpent is wisdom moving through the body. An arrow shot into the throat clears the passage, establishing a bridge between realms. Here is the ladder, the angels ascending and descending at will.

The second shot would have further opened the passage, or perhaps closed it off, my plaint drawing the baleful and malign.

conscience. We cannot reason with Adam's mind.

AT THE END, ADAM

There is nothing but the drift of ash, a sky falling, human-made light rising from a body as we the fireflies ascend, we the fireflies in the meadow, the beauty of light with no will but to be taken.

Blessed are the meek, it is written. Therefore, I'm ending us to begin again, ending in love, for what I see of God is not here. There are some so removed from the world as to be the world's existence and its end.

I speak. I tell you not as victim, no, not timorously but boldly, as one who has gone to an angel and entered him from within, touched that we now fly this Human land.

BOOK 6

And [the Rulers] erred, not knowing that it was their own body that they had defiled: it was the likeness that the authorities and their angels defiled in every way.

ON THE ORIGIN OF THE WORLD

IN THE POUNDINGS, THE PROMISE OF WHAT SHINES

Whatever it was within me tilting my body to the side, slipped free from my arm and was gone. Light and love gone now, swept from my body in a creature departing. What have I done?

Emptiness full of self, full now of this heavy earth self who knows nothing but regret and lack in a dying world of which she's now a part.

What a shot to the throat renders silent cannot be undone, and still I come to you. How could I? Barren and empty are antitheses, one quite full.

There are some so attuned to the darkness they can see the things that are.

The god passes. I feel oldness that is not mine, a sense that I have always been. Human sadness, failure. My pleas to you resound in commonness, nothing profound in the ululation. Take me back. Let me know light again even through the darkness.

Fall, fall through yourself: a voice, a memory of my own.

I WILL CALL YOU ADAM

I am in retrograde. Teach me. I have fallen back into this body again, sealed the tomb at my center. I cannot feel. I do not understand what you would have me do. How I tire, God. How I tire God. How I tire and yet push blindly on. Would that you moved my heart. Would that I weren't so small, so human. You have stripped me of word, set the lexicon, too, in retrograde, so that I am dumb, human, toy.

The ones who know darkness, the ones who know light, of nonduality sing, a bell clanging above. And so I sing in the silence God's name, for I am the eternal darkness of light. I am the light in the darkness. I am the light. Glass, ember, an angel slipping its hands around my heart, its hands holding a flame, a bleeding ember.

∞

I have come too far to return. I stagger into Manley's arms, head heavy with snake. I will call you Adam, I say.

aurora. There is no precedent for this.
conscience. What you have done.

∞

conscience. Did you think you were alone in the stairwell? Did you think you were ever alone with the light?

aurora. Then what of my heart box? What of the elixir?

conscience. It is your blood. Light has no container. Concentrated, it has properties that can leak out, but they dissipate and all is one light. Form obscures this. Semblance obfuscates vision. What did you think you would do with it?

aurora. I had heard stories about a drop, so that I could feel it, could see it within me contained within a brass pyx, a tabernacle at the center of my chest, held within a vial, and it was green this elixir of life. I imagined I could heal the earth with it, give strength to the natural realm that it might cure the devastation reeked by Human. Why don't I count myself part of this?

conscience. Because you are not. Give voice to what is within you. It is less what we do here externally than how we develop from within.

aurora. I was not to notice its passing.

conscience. Think of the realms beneath this one. How you went to the bird and tried to save it. But Human Aurora, the Human realm.

aurora. When we maim and destroy?

conscience. Forgo judgment.

ELIJAH

conscience. Tell of the sky we drew for you last night, the night before; how God speaks to each in her own language, how beauty might be a tree blossoming in the head; how a snake might be harbinger, an external sign alerting you to what you'd ever conceived; how one might be visited by the eternals, these wise men who'd come; and how her own dragon, her own tyrannical ruler might conjure a one to tamp out the light and make us run; how the way back might elude us, the heart chakra leaked and coffer bound; and how we'd go on. So it is we live and die, Elijah. Have I not come for the end? Have I not come? And so to save a world would end us.

aurora. You have ways I know not of. I see myself far in the distance, across a mystic plane, and yet no assemblage could capture what fleets when defined, the illusive might of one in dream and collusion.

conscience. Collusion?

aurora. Collusion with God. We are. We die here, and I am killing us. I cannot help it. I am Elijah, fire begotten. I have asked you for stream, a pot, anvil, horn. I have asked for a handle and spade. I have been swept clean of ambition. Self-righteous, I wait.

Is this the meekness of which you speak?

And what do you know of the orb wavering on its post? The animal form, what has left the world annexed, exiled, re-bled? I have asked to see everything.

This is not a story. There are some among us. Bring me through. I will summon the wind, await no storm. Fire will blaze at my command.

conscience. Elijah, put down the sword.

EGO RESURGENCE

Something in the inverted world's gone wrong. Pressure in my skull, a brain swollen for Ego wills it on and on. Finish before the poison sets in. I have been a failure in this world of men.

God, I lay my body down. I relinquish all to your might, for I am mere transcriber of a dream, an instrument you mend in the night.

And on the morrow, the head held aslant in the light, how she'd intimate a walk, how we'd get outside, and she would slip out my arm and be gone from me.

conscience. What if this were growth, Aurora, increasing the capacity to comprehend, to organize and order what you have done? Consciousness expanding, unfolding, and unfurling that you might see.

aurora. Thy will and not mine be done.

conscience. Our will is the same. God cannot bestow on you what you cannot imagine to you belongs. "From those who have not will be taken even that which they have."

aurora. Rintrah's heart is my heart. The jays chant their assent, while the wild woman grins from the card. Let wisdom writhe in the brain until it stretches us capable of carrying the sun: light of comprehension, light of peace. Cast its beams in what direction?

conscience. In the direction those deem from where

you've come, the Eternals ever within, a council of the righteous.

Aurora, get to the tree.

THE SERPENT AS GIFT

Shhhhh. This one is quiet, her voice a serpent through the brush, ubiquitous: a warning undecipherable to the virgin ear. Cast a glance westward through hickory and pine, raise a foot to mount the granite slab, this cracked door allotment, and the rattler uncoils in the cool crepuscule on a ridge overlooking the sky. How it folds into a letter, a cuneiform prepared to strike: a world in a letter, a warning at dawn. How action might contain language, lexicon, word. How the world, too much with us, might become reticent—how I in casting my attention within might have silenced it for a while that the snake might come with a message, that this might be the last, the final of three.

I am still. My body is sunlight half an hour to dawn, my pores, every atom a particle of light. There is peace within my breast, for my breast is a coffer, and this coffer belongs to God. It is metal, it is glass, it is wood, or did it only begin like this? Wood, the house at the edge of winter, glass, where we'd kept the girl, metal, the angel's vestment and his shield.

Father, Father, the loon has gotten out. The ring has gone foul around the moon...

Voices come. We will have a story.

What will I restore?

aurora. Light in shadow. Flint in the dark walls of the

carven, a cave going nowhere at the end of a world. Turn the light.

conscience. Shhhhh. Quiet the mind. Write the story of God, Aurora. Write the world that dwells within and beyond.

aurora. A pulse of light, a synaptic firing in the wings. If one turn the light on a world and all that she knew...

The heart box pops in expansion, a cow bulldozed across a floor. I will break. I will die here, my heart a cow heart, a hide broken open on the edge of a shovel.

conscience. Shhhhh. Quiet the heart, love.

aurora. But they are mine, these creatures. If I were to break into a thousand shards...

Oh the repercussions on a cosmic form. They know not what they do. What we do to others we've endured. Oh wake up. Within there is a voice that suffers long.

∞

There is conclusion based on trajectory, and then there is Wisdom, what knows I am not to change this. The universe is abundant. We will be reborn. But to save her...

We save ourselves.

I BECOME THE TREE

conscience. Aurora, the light.

aurora. Brighter against the darkness.

conscience. You'll be harmed. You'll draw us back along the perpetual. Lift your head from your tale. Tell me what you see in the light, in the ones you hold in counsel, what will come. Concentrate on the light in the stars.

aurora. Come then. It is almost night. A tree unfurls its leaves in the darkness against a tar black sky, and there in the distance chips of light fall like embers from the black-smith's pipe.

Aphids in the daylight blight the crook of branch. Hear the tinkle of song in their movement, a suite in a forest sweetly ravaging all in white, while ashen mold seeps into the floor all around.

conscience. Tell me who you are.

aurora. The one who sees these things and cannot turn away, so that I become the tree and the aphids and ash on a forest floor. What is more, I have ever been and left these grounds. Unlatch the coffer, a doll drops out. The coffer is lead; its plate doors swing forward as I'm tipped.

Blake? I have gotten old in a dream. Tilt my brazen head. Let me hear what the council is saying.

Deliberation deliberating, deliberate.

I have seen. One moves through the trees. There is an end to flight.

I am nodding off. I fall into sleep: the grief god come in a gust that takes us from the pernicious. Merciful fingers steeped in confection, a thumb depresses my tongue. Water in the chalice of my head. It is like this for some.

The desire to know grows us, these plates in the head moving tectonic, what I once thought depression: a godhead preparing the one on the ground. I am here. My gown red where the leaves were torn. All that I didn't know now I know. Sleeper. Dream angel, I know you in gold, Centurion. What would I drink of an arrow? I am whoever receives me. Whoever. Stretch my skull. Come. Make it impossible for me to be small.

Unfurling, unfurling, the sky is mine, but I have not caught fire. The words have not caught fire. Cerebral all. I know without the heart, she bled.

How many times I have been here, plates within the skull colliding, forming I know not what beauty. I am under your protection within the egg of supernal flow. It is why time. It is why I wait now, an inlet, portal, door to Human. The one on the ground ready...

conscience. And yet so torn and fragmented.

aurora. In my chest, vacancy not yet formed. An angel making reparations, a stave of light. Use my body to scrape the stars. Those we left on the rocks will die. Our covenant this. What erodes my skin, what sheathes in fascicles, what tree whose bark erodes, whose trunk, whose stem an ivory column, a flume.

Beauty writhes; plankton catches fire. What can be touched what resonates in fathoms what traverse time in flesh flame.

I slip in the heart blood. I am a bird, ribbon frayed.

AND THE GODS CAME DOWN

My voice weeps. There it is fabric, silken and frayed. A ribbon tied to a bird. There it catches the light and does not burn but go out. I will go to the one within I have harmed, the soul again stillborn, but no, aborted in diatribe. How can I say this? How can I say it is not?

What is mine? What is yours? Is ours? I wait. My instrument dry. Chords, cords, cords of birds. Sanguine. A ribbon heavy with blood, blood that has coagulated bordeaux along the seams where thread has loosened and released. I will play and be played. With what artistry, with what precision what you have done. A human gorge. A Badland. Time: the wind's hands. How many times have I been here? The last scene. That we be no more. A dying human. An animal form. The gown hung before me in the light.

Some of us...

Laurel clusters drowned and tipped. What energy moves through my head, the crown extending outward as chalice, a receptacle filled with water, yet more viscous. Mind fluid, flowing into mind, that mind be emotion. What can be defined? What value reason? I call out science, the prosaic, defunct opossum. What have you done?

Beauty as mine fathoms long. When I speak you will know me, for I have been in the desert. Light, let there be light again. Elijah, let there be light not lit with bomb.

Stay your hand now. Stay your head. It is right that we've come.

Do you see in the deep blue chinks in the armor of night God's darkness? I am in the dream a soporific hymn; my walls are fluid, my head fluid. I walk in sleep knowing the walls to be cloud, what I might sense beyond what I might conjure or draw forth or know.

My voice is the voice of the mountains, this migrant bird. Will it be all right if I show you?

Oh who are you serpent carving out my path? Love, charged and charging through my head!

∞

In the myth, there is a forest of branchless trees, stalk-dry.

There is only clarity. There is only God.

aurora. Give me a rod. Time has come for ease. I have been through everything. Take me out, or let me be. What good is seeing if none hear. Cassandra, Jeremiah, Elijah.

conscience. Eve, Aurora. Eve.

ELIJAH

I will not sleep, and if I do not sleep, I will not lose you.
My God, what I will not do of myself in a night. Tyrant.
Child. When one knew. But I do not know what is ex-
pected. I would tear off the skin. My heart is broken, all
replete with light, a skill, a meekness. What if the one
sent did not make it past the stable? Those who came to
look on. Did I get it wrong? Were they sent to harm, to
hinder my passage? I feel what truth belies. I am a ham-
mer. I will not survive.

And yet if I were to tell the story as I know it in my
heart. Elijah, you tell me, Elijah. I hear from the cliff face,
from the orchard. Who could stop Elijah but God?

conscience. Use the energy for what it was bestowed.
aurora. You've given me no means. I have a soul of
toys, a heart box bled. And yet I saw how something lu-
minous might unveil and transcend.
conscience. Cast off the mortal being. Watch at the
cusp where paper blackens so dark it could only be
brightness.

∞

There is a tear now in the heart box. How the wind
might get in if I let it, how the heart might be bled on a
mountain.

What must it feel like to pierce with beak a metal lid? I am not like these things of world.

WE BELONG TO SOMETHING

My beauty is in breaking on the cusp: a human fallen and a soul like a shade slipped over the light. I am not afraid of what Human does in drifting drifting drifting. I am come.

A paroxysm of sweetness sweeps through my body. Happiness leaks through the cracks in my face, fissures, brine-eroded, my jaw quivering as if I were cold. We belong to something. I try to outrun it gleefully, but the violent shuddering hangs on down the dirt road and around the bend.

aurora. I wasn't to notice its passing but what?
conscience. What we'd be not being Human.
aurora. Last night after making love to Manley, tears flowed, and your voice returned.
conscience. Yes, the beauty of the human animal.
aurora. I know it gone, your presence affirmation that we end. What I have chosen. Our bodies an emanation of the beautiful, the divine, chosen as we would choose unconsciously to express beauty in a form, love a form, ourselves a form. And then that form might need to grow, and we would grow it. Conscience would grow it. Out of necessity, we would grow.

world. Who are you?
aurora. The one to show we have gotten it wrong.

There is a God, hands pressed to the glass of the sky. A wolf, its face a handprint, howls.

Wind on water all exuding light. Crescent moon atop crescent moon. Figures rise in the foreground, climbing the embankment laden with pack.

They take us out sometimes, the eternals. I find myself lost in time, hours I can't explain. We have chosen this, to be wrought so, eroded, supped.

THE SPIDER

The spider forges an auspicious way through the sky, and I am in love with you, God, reverently and hopelessly in love with the beauty threaded through trees in light. Peace. No words, heart box clasped tight.

There is humbleness which emboldens, that passion felt at the base of the tree to be quiet reverence. No words. I have no words for this. How when we don't move we become assimilated into a hill covered gossamer. Wings in warning. The childlike feeling of belong.

I sit in the light, and rainbows form in my hair, within the follicle a cosmos of stars. Here an ancient riddle. How is it light reveals the internal structure, cells as if magnified before me. Segment on segment in circular form. I strain my eyes, and light moves on.

EGO AND THE TREE

aurora. Blood, and I sense a battle has ensued in the night, for I wake with my head on fire, the root ends pinched and squeezed dry, contracting with my thought, shutting out sustenance. My ears are bleeding. How can a tree bleed? For this is not sap but blood, clearly wounds at the seams where flesh was torn.

conscience. You have cut at it in the night to save us from punishment.

aurora. My skull is battered. My mouth bleeds from its ceiling, the vortex, cathedral. How can I release the tyrant over these things, this lower mind that says I must perform?

conscience. Shhhhh. Be still.

aurora. What would unfurl in my throat is smattered against the sides like an insect. Blood and swelling along the neck. They think we are mad.

conscience. Shhhh. Rest. No more. You can no longer reason with Adam's mind. It destroys you. The veins have swollen, swell. Blood trickles from your ears. You have wrung out your brain. You are wringing him out. Feel the fire of friction. What would have you stop is saying...

∞

Vertigo when I surface and pain that asks me to seek its source again. I feel something tug on my jaw, swelling

77

and tearing further into tissue.

Maybe this is part of the regeneration process, but I sense more my resistance destroys, as Ego holds to earthly form.

HUMAN SILENCED

The mystic speaks not to Human but as she was spoken to, soul in soul's language, Human silenced. There is no guilt; there is only knowing and unknown.

An angel casts his pink shade before the sky, and I am to take his hand and walk or fly.

What need would God have for fearing a man? Zoe, rise. I have erred.

My heart neither full nor empty, feeling not but the metal clasp against my flesh cold hang like an emblem, a trinket on a chain, a pendulum asked what will.

aurora. Wisdom is this your plane? For I feel no longer peace, but peace.
conscience. Did you think this wasn't real? It is yours because you see.

How I know darkness to be light in its polarity and so wisdom at its height.
Let go, I hear not in voice but cognized that word reaches my heart. That if we let go we'd fall into divine order, into peace and happiness, within and without, inner and outer one. How I know this and still cannot. How can I let go of Adam?

VISION

There is a horned figure in chiaroscuro, a half-face peering from behind another, the one in profile, textured like a brain. A stream of liquid pours from his upper lip, breaking the surface of the ground, so that it becomes a branch on which the man's face is braced. What appeared brain becomes half tree, the bridge of the devil's nose a torso, the socket protruding above the eye, an arm. The figure covers its face with one hand while the other is held up in offering; a snake runs parallel, mimicking the gesture. Or is it another arm?

One horn is a crescent moon, the other a gown.

In my hand is the dark form of a child: a star that has stopped shining. The branch and trunk are its legs. It is dancing, Bacchanal, a sash of fire low on its waist.

aurora. What are you saying?

conscience. The devil is composure; the man he becomes frantic and blind, in other words, the god obscured in the second face, for all is God.

As soon as we look around this world of forms for what is allowed, we lose sight of our power. Never adapt for lower Human, or conform.

You are the tree.

∞

In the dream, a fox cavorts up a hill, its pelt undulating in the light racing across its body. It arcs wide around me then collapses at my back. A fawn follows frangibly through the tall grasses as a moose emerges from the thicket in pursuit. Fatigable, the fawn leaps and falls, leaps and falls, and one hears what might be its legs crumbling beneath it. Finally, it drops behind me beside the fox. And then the moose, overrun with exhaustion, harrows a patch as it, too, falls. I turn and watch the erratic respiration quiet as all repose.

How in dream wisdom takes hold of the unconscious that she might know the creatures to be herself running from the world and seeking refuge in herself.

∞

A horse with tired eyes laps at the ground. While providence shines on him from above. On his back are plants. Symbiosis, a wading bird. Serpents. The world on his back. He wearies. He has stopped drinking. World pierces the hide. His legs tenuous. His eye a cross. Above his fourth leg, in the scrotum is seed, a circle, or orb, something contained.

∞

A small dark form walks toward a dark wood. The sky is falling slowly, assiduously, roiling and turning over above the dark form. An aura encircles him. God is a figure half dark, half bright. In his brightness, a lion, a man, a paw holding open the sky.
The sky is a rippling mane.

The figure is sent.

The dark side of God is a bird in profile, its open beak of the lion's nose and mouth composed. Sound waves travel out over the sky in visible form.

The lion's eye sees all, the lion's paw grips the edge of sky. It is in its power. It is. And the bird. They are in balance and powerfully extant. Light comes in two beams from above, but the figure doesn't notice the light. He thinks he is alone on his journey. The lion holds strong.

The forest becomes the shadows of the Eternals nodding their heads and urging the figure on. How small and perfect his task. How below is a darkness where we all are born. How small and necessary the embryonic night. How long.

I am in the lion.

His, my mouth, my nose, my eyes.

Let me be the lion, no longer human. But I am everything and in all.

Love could be a star inside you, leaping into the room where you are, catching on and illuminating a realm within this one, so that all you thought to be real faded to the extent that your body glowed. And in that light was peaceful bliss, your body lucence without form. Remember your human body, a semblance of flesh that levitates now, glides buoyant through life. Human is a body you inhabit, a garment, a city to be burned.

conscience. Oh Aurora, we took the souls that you might see and turn from specter, Adam's soulless world.

THE MYSTIC CHARGE

Within is wisdom, and I know how many times I have
been here, how long I have slept in the skull, how God is
the sweetness of phenomena, what in my chest weeps for
us, what I instill in empty form.

My head nods. How can I be and not be here? How can
we stretch our toes and extend our limbs until we exceed
the space of Human, its limitation, its poverty? What
must I relinquish but world? A world of illusion born of
error. It was in sacrificing self that I was born into light.
Yet that light is gone, the portal sealed, and the way back
never the same. How could it be? The body defends
against pain. How enter knowingly what harms?

By altering the future I change the past. Conversely, by
altering the past, I change the future. Consciousness on
another plane. I send the birds. I send the light beings. I
send prosperity, love.

But it is not like this. All exists at one time. Therefore,
we change nothing. All exists simply. Each state we fall
into or rise from exists. I am. I am consciousness. What I
am conscious of exists as a body, a world grown out of be-
liefs. Our error was in identifying ourselves with the form
and so becoming entrapped by it, contained.

To believe in worldly systems enslaves us, Adam. It is
to place phenomena over God. Rest in the light and know
all. Rest in the light of truth and know the world to be

kindness. Know the world to be love. Know God to be the light within. The fall was both of us, Adam. Oh to know wisdom, to be wisdom, to know no harm, no adverse thing or force. I remember. As light our body is wisdom, and wisdom the body of all. That I associate you with the physical, that I align you with external forces and so what is opposed to me and to the principles of truth, divides us, but you too are my soul and you too err as I err when I believe in worldly limitation.

For you to see would be death... But you could not.

And perhaps because I was not ready for you to see me like this, the light has left me. I shoved her down, my wings, my beauty. I understand now that I did not know how to exist, and so it was ever me, the world we believed in.

To see truth is to leave the illusion.

EVERY STORY IS ONE OF OUR BEGINNNING

What we are, what I see that cannot be adulterated or caged is what without a pure spirit or bright heart, what without reverence, one can never know.

Every story is one of our beginning. One says come, brave the unknown. The path is mutable; the portal itself ruse. Alice again. Every story our story. I am, and through my head movement: something shifts, conscious. As I write I am drawing into existence what always was.

Time circumscribes. Remove its constraints: vision eternal.

Chamuel in pink light sets the sky ablaze.

That we might jumpstart the heart by running, by falling, relinquishing hard, feeling at the polarity of sensation, a cusp ever a seam ever a portal where one can see through antithetical properties the nonduality in all, where one can enter in or destroy. At the extremes, what we are made aware of becomes us.

It is never the same way to the light, never the same way down inside. In this way, the heart must grow. In this way, we assure the purity of the traveler, the heroic one. In this state I cannot carry a failed heart, what is leaked and void. Yet I see what is empty for its fullness.

To say it was like this for one, that your world has failed and will fail again but for those with their eyes toward the stars, those to whom phenomena eternally recurs as a play, those who have stepped beyond scrim into the unseen.

∞

I have spilled the liquid. Oh how cold where the light gapes around the wound in black star.

What if I've been depleted? What if I haven't the strength, light stolen and leaked, to go on?

In the story you bring him light. It is this that restores the soul.

Sleep again. Dhyana. Who is speaking but a memory of what comes?

NOT HUMAN

As soon as I transfer consciousness to the five husbands,
I am Human again, a shell, a body with a job, not mine. A
wooden form, a body dangles from a crucifix. Webs, and
my arms are entangled, for who would move the puppet
must step back from the stage and see the spectacle of all.

THE BENEFICENT

I see her then the black bird, my companion of the crepuscule, the internal queen whispering in the alcoves.
This world is breaking me. My nerves quiver. My arms are
a floor of scorpions or crabs. What I have done is spill the
elixir.

conscience. You will have to make it alone.

But my arms flee, and my heart box metals against my
flesh, nothing to burn but liquid. No other gods before
God.

∞

aurora. If I could, this would be the scene in which the
beneficent won out.
conscience. Beneficent always wins out: the one in
your head who swims, whose motion causes tremors
through your jaw, the water rocking your skull in palsy,
and your right arm numb, and the dream in which you
are called to ascend and your body is held aloft in the
light, you levitating, the center buoyant in love. Outside
of you is a story of a human life.
aurora. I have only vacancy in my heart and a memory
of a strand where I was taken and wrung. How long can
one exist in her own cave? How long stand at the

entrance? A red bird in flight chuffing up and out her mouth. Take me out in death, or let me live ever in communion, a covenant sustaining us. Let me move so far beyond material existence as to shine again, as to be the light, for I know too much to be Human. If I can draw from the bottom of the world this light, if one return with it. If one return.

My head is heavy and viscous.

The blue jay shrieks imitable in my branches.

Will you call me into the pool again of the unmaechtig? I feel the tug of sleep. Where then do I go? How I have robbed myself by failing to recognize there might have been a path had I imagined it. To silence the lion that I might continue. All things are possible to God.

We seek the light that is our salvation. And yet the light is ourselves shining when we relinquish ourselves to God, to our divine nature. I have come too far to return. I will be led by what knows me at my beginning and end.

White flakes of light chipped from the space around me turn in the wind. Stars coming in and out of existence, tiring. A particle appearing, disappearing.

conscience. Don't step back in.

aurora. I can't now. The room is full of them, what has come, and I am being lifted in the light. I float here. I levitate.

Until the lion comes whose presence catapults me to the floor.

IN RATIO TO DESIRE

Before the window is God; God, where my mind reaches the height of ascension. Only form surrounds, form with no power but what I assign to it, no value but what value I assign. I am that I am outside the constraints of Human, beyond in a place where all is possible, for all is possible to God.

"There are things you can't understand, Adam, things I cannot tell you."
"For example?"
"You'd break them."
—
"The skull grows in ratio to its desire."
—
"The more we seek in reverence of what is natural and true and good, the more we grow and the larger our capacity for apprehension. We have only to turn enough away from the world of phenomena and into the world of darkness (light) to know it, to see and to remember. Wisdom is there: what I am conscious of being, the wise one within me. I am past future, world beyond time on a plane of light. I am more than this world of phenomena, and yet existing within it I am able to conjure and move and cloister and surround. Will you know me? Will you want to know me?"

REGENERATION

In the back of my throat, where the angel shot the arrow is a pewter wedge, a round slab, something metal and dense and expanding, something fluid and dark.

Energy moves my head, winding me as a wheel, tightening the thread, winding and winding a metallic cord on a spool until I am an instrument, until I feel the string taut and my head tipped low onto another strand, another wheel dipping and circling.

There is fire to the left of my face, a creature grazing my cheek. From the outside, bodies enter the space before me, nearly touching their faces to mine as they peer into my visage. Somehow the angel... What will I sing? What we are, this metal cord, this energy, strained and expanding.

∞

The animals raced out of the forest and laid themselves down at my back. They had run a long time, their tired breath percussive, a song lifting something within me that was to be their guardian. And they on the lawn of my heart, cleaved and so reluctant: a ravaged lute the song repairs.

BOOK 7

When god created me out of the earth along with your mother Eve, I went about with her in a glory that she saw in the eternal realm from which we came. She taught me knowledge of the eternal god. And we resembled the great eternal angels, for we were higher than the god who created us and the powers with him, whom we did not know.

THE REVELATION (APOCALYPSE) OF ADAM

THE REVELATION OF EVE

Rainbows fill the sky on each thin cloud. If you could see, you could not destroy and yet, still chained to the beast, I writhe. What caps the head but limitations, misconceptions of a Human mind.

I see them as dead and remove them, Wisdom ever the serpent, Human ever the creation, what came of a one who thought herself divine.

Oh, what was it that James said in the apocrypha? That this was no err but a process of expansion. Again my heart is distant, and these words lithe. Beneath the cap one listens. There is strange compression, an unevenness and something lifting off the back of my psychic skull, something tugging at the roots within the loam, holding my head from a thick cord, a branch or bough, a vine. I see it thick and beige. What fruit this? What vegetable? Ahhh, like a radish tail, a giant root, loosening the soil. And within my head the seed and hollow darkness, the black expanse of what in vacancy forms.

Wisdom, I see what would corrupt of this world and ask for your protection. A hand reaches my hand and something metal and cold is deposited there. It grows warm, this white metal that bifurcates the space all around. In tandem, the metal skull cap warms and spreads, and from the back of my head the armor slips down.

What of the vine suspended? I do not feel. There is

throbbing in my left lobe. Would that this simulacra did not beat through at times, did not sound in my body and mind. To hear it as God's voice, this clanging, and not to fear what an Archon could create of dust.

Come. In stillness. I will fetch the animals, the ones who come to me at dusk, the foxes in darkness. Red cry the young, each peal, a face in the pleroma.

I love, and the heart is a word I have been given, entrusted as a gift, and I am here forever waiting on the dawn, the covenant promised. Staid, the purple hand, and the glove that breathes of fire through my hair. I will bare my serpents and you the purple hand, and we will rise and rise and rise through the dawn, this gray ball at my center inflating in the light, this disk hacked from throat, what makes me weak to the insurgence of disease, what takes my voice and thins the cords, or powders them, or plays them like an instrument strummed raw, so that they ache at times, so that I weep at the world's song, for it is so full of darkness.

We pass the light, James, and I know you've gone this way before. Damp breath through the alcove. Ragged wet. (Stay down, and you mean inside of you. Inside of me. A name, elusive. A name I would call you, but you have none.) And in the room a handful of shadows, conversing and smearing the surface with what is not real, what in distraction wears a label of dissatisfying green. An orange t-shirt. An ensnaring grin. A campus of herded aspirations and me on the lawn seeing everything, my chest torn to the blue sky, idyllic light, ethereal cast, for we were beyond, and beyond the light is kind.

What drops the temperature of body allows something else to move in. Body dies and spirit sinks in the draft.

Why would we pollute what we can't understand?

It was a snare, my Adam. They would never let you leave once you'd arrived, once they'd crowned you and given you the whore.

I am she. And I am not afraid to claim you in thighs that wrap the world and coddle the head of the serpent. For what are we Adam but a dream of gods creating dreams? If we stay here, death. If we stay, they have incorporated us into their system. We have no mind of our own but the mind they control. Can't you see, Adam? Can't you hear?

Finish your story.

But who says this? Adam, is it you? Sometimes God takes and speaks through you, amplifying your beauty in the light. It is this Adam that I love.

But I cannot stop this desecration, not by my will. It is why some were chosen, that we do not interfere or apply force to things. Commanding is your way, not mine. Your way is killing the ones we need. Come, take my hand. We will go together.

Adam. Into death?

Aurora. Into what is real, never to return to the place of lack.

Past the blue curve of the earth, my head bobs like a galleon on a sea of protean depth. We rise and fall. The wreck of the Deutschland with a scent as bland as habit. And still we rise and fall, dipping into the sea's black light. We circle around and watch the sky. How many others coiled like this on the serpent's back? What I ask is given. Where are the ones like me?

How a whore might not be soiled but more pure for the hands that touched her touched her not. Zoe, wake up. It was not our body but a body made. There is light and there is darkness. When one knows both, she transcends harm.

"The soul in us, being in itself beautiful, rejoices in beholding its own likeness in other things."

Plotinus

Our error was in thinking ourselves divided. Our error was in imagining a world divided from the light. We are light indivisible, the unbegotten, the unmade. Know this and what manifests will be in love.

Pass through to here, however, and what we have done will no longer recognize itself. It will enter a realm of falsehood, of fear, of envy in which what rises up dies.

In God we live and move and have our being. A world unfolds within a world. I am inverted in the light; the inner realm manifesting on the stage of form, incorruptible and true, for as long as I exist undivided from the light, as long as I am aware of existing undivided from the light, as long as I am conscious of what is true, the external body manifests true form.

To remain in the consciousness of the light is to remember it only. We woke, and the sky was our sky, the sky we made. We recognized ourselves in its pure beauty, its gift of life. All was self. There was nothing that was not kindness, nothing that felt other than me. I was breath. I was the air. My body was the day. There was nothing that I touched that touched me not and yet I was purity in form, ether.

I try again to breathe the golden light through this body and to ascertain what you are asking of me when I would be you. When I know at my heart that I am this silent stillness, this peace, and I would rest in it until it grew powerful again and spread itself through the room and through the cosmos, and I would be the consciousness within it. And I would settle back and know how love might move one.

What defines itself as Human can do little here.

not human

The bird was the world, and I was the light of god breathing life into its dying form. Because I saw that I could, because I saw that this was the light's purpose.

two worlds

"How long halt ye between two opinions? If the Lord be God, then follow him, but if Baal, then follow him."
1 Kings 18:21

God, I am at your feet, and at your feet I am an angel taking to flight with its powerful wings. What is façade, what is unrighteous I leave on the ground as I ascend to the heights once again.

And I understand now what before I had not, that I am not above body as a ruling force. I exist instead within an organism which when it rests in love, lives in the perfect state of peace. Light radiates through its surround and shadows disappear. It was the shadow that was the Governors' realm, an illusion that cannot exist in light. Therefore, I must not contend with these things of world. I must not conjure or appeal to their rule.

I come from above. I do not bend but ask you to rise.

this is my body

All that recreates the surface is in error; all that perpetuates a system of tyranny and lack reinforces an illusion and strengthens a vision that never was. Only God: the wedding of sun and moon.

And so I am not asked to be Human, not even asked to rise from Human or evolve. I must simply enter what is true and explore it until the parameters of my vision expand and in this expansion a world evolves. I am not an imperfect and suffering being, dragging itself around and healing in time. What exists within can do everything now.

We touch the cosmic realm and return so that dreams remain in a realm apart and can do nothing here, but what if here did not exist but as an idea I kept conjuring, an imperfect idea.

the time of adam's rule is over

There is no Father in Eve. Do not accept what is below you to think, to conceive, only because it has been. The time of Adam's rule is over. The black mag is the source of your power. She is fierce in a way love is fierce, in the way it is absolute. There is no tolerance in the black mag, no dowdiness, no rest. She does not cow-tow or tip toe around. And yet I say she. Yes, she, what you ever relegated to the darkness. You will need it all. What in truth transforms. What in light scathes, the way it vanquishes the darkness, so that nothing can exist but it, what is true, what loves, what in and of itself propagates.

Rise. There is no sadness. There is no sentiment or

maudlin parting. There is only what in the darkness of birth knows herself.

I see it still in the distance, still in the haze of preconception, this cosmic golden form, what is eternal night, eternal day, what has no parameter, no end. But the beginning is ever within.

the second mystery

To remain within the form is to die with the body, to suffer its trauma, its plight. To recognize that we are not the body but that the body is an apparatus and extension of our thoughts is to rise above form into what is not bound to physical law, what is free of the hypostasis of the archons. What is the body of all.

I am the second mystery, what begins ever one unbegotten then falls into division by her own hand. By what desire we fall is the desire to love only, which is then corrupted by form. Division. We must only remember the light; return to truth to see it.

Who would understand would need to hear with the ears of the spirit, for here the umbrage of the whole rises into consciousness. We see not an aspect of story but the impetus within, ever this rising into the light of wisdom, peace, perfect beauty. Let yourself go with me and know the rest that manifests a kingdom without a king. What would hold you captive is only misunderstanding, a shade before the light.

the self in God

I cannot fall here. Buoyant in love, I cannot fail. And so let there be no other. Let there be no error, no veil. No vulnerability even. Oh love what would touch you touches all. Breathe in and know the breath is God, God the body, God the floor. God the squirrel and the tree, the seeds you scatter, the man on the ground before you. Do not segregate or relegate or separate divide, but enter the soul and know your desire to love infused through all. Love only. And know the body of love; flight, this adroit bird aloft arching her wings and settling down, and these vultures their wings at various stages of opening. One stretched and drying, what is dying consumed. How they urinate on their feet to cleanse them. How we work together autonomously. How what I might sense might lead you to the carrion where you will feast.

Moisten your feet in the dead ones. Rise and dry your wings. I am the sunlight. I am flight. I am the self in God.

I have not brought peace but a sword

to behead the world of John.

Made in United States
North Haven, CT
27 June 2023

38286983R00065